Oxygen

and the Group 6 Elements

Nigel Saunders

Heinemann
LIBRARY

www.heinemann.co.uk/library
Visit our website to find out more information about Heinemann Library books.

To order:
 Phone 44 (0) 1865 888066
 Send a fax to 44 (0) 1865 314091
 Visit the Heinemann Bookshop at www.heinemann.co.uk/library to browse our catalogue and order online.

First published in Great Britain by Heinemann Library, Halley Court, Jordan Hill, Oxford OX2 8EJ, part of Harcourt Education.
Heinemann is a registered trademark of Harcourt Education Ltd.

Editorial: Sarah Eason and Kathy Peltan
Design: David Poole and
    Tinstar Design Limited (www.tinstar.co.uk)
Illustrations: Geoff Ward and Paul Fellows
Picture Research: Rosie Garai
Production: Viv Hichens
Originated by Blenheim Colour Ltd
Printed and bound in Hong Kong and China by
    South China.

ISBN 0 431 16983 7
07 06 05 04 03
10 9 8 7 6 5 4 3 2 1

British Library Cataloguing in Publication Data
Saunders, Nigel
    Oxygen and the group 6 elements
    523.8
A full catalogue record for this book is available from the British Library.

Acknowledgements
The publishers would like to thank the following for permission to reproduce photographs:
Corbis pp**4**, **8** (Roger Ressmeyer), **28** (Robin Adshead The Military Picture Library), **50** (Wes Thompson); Getty Images (Inc. Archive Holdings) p**19**; Holt Studios (Nigel Cattlin) p**47**; Peter Evans p**24**; Peter Morris pp**38**, **40**; Redferns p**31**; Royal Pump Room Museum, Harrogate p**39**; Science Photo Library pp**9** (Bernhard Edmaier), **10** (G.Brad Lewis), **15** top left (David Taylor), **15** top right (Charles D. Winters), **15** bottom (David Parker), **21** (Charles D. Winters), **22** (Deep Light Productions), **27** (Rosenfeld Images Ltd) **29** (Nasa), **32** (Francoise Sauze), **35** (Steve Horrell), **42** (David Taylor), **48** (C.S. Langlois, Publiphoto Diffusion), **53** (Russ Lappa), **56** (Stanley B. Burns, MD & The Burns Archive N.Y.), **57** (Novosti); Trevor Clifford p**20**; Trip (Helen Rogers) pp**45**, **55**.

Cover photograph of bubbles, reproduced with permission of Alamy

The author would like to thank Angela, Kathryn, David and Jean for all their help and support.

The publishers would like to thank Alexandra Clayton for her assistance in the preparation of this book.

Disclaimer

Contents

Words appearing in bold, **like this**, are explained in the Glossary

CHAPTER 1

Elements and atomic structure

If you look around, you'll see metals, plastics, water and lots of other solids and liquids. You cannot see the gases in the air, but you know they are there along with many other gases too. Incredibly, over 19 million different substances have been discovered, named and catalogued. About 4000 more substances are added to the list every day, yet all of these are made from just a few simple building blocks called **elements**.

Elements

There are 92 naturally occurring elements and a few artificial ones, including element number 116 in group 6. An element is a substance that cannot be broken down into simpler materials using chemical **reactions**. About three-quarters of the elements are metals, such as iron and polonium, and most of the rest are non-metals, such as oxygen and sulphur. Some elements, like tellurium, are called metalloids because they have some of the properties of metals and some of the properties of non-metals.

Compounds

Compounds are made when elements join together in chemical reactions. For example, iron sulphide is made when iron and sulphur react together, and sulphur dioxide is made when sulphur and oxygen react together. There are countless ways in which two or more elements can join together to make compounds. This means that nearly all of the millions of different substances in the world are compounds.

When the space shuttle lifts ▶ off from the Kennedy Space Centre in Florida, its fuel tanks are full of chemicals that combine together to release enough energy to launch it into space.

Atoms

Every substance is made up of tiny particles called **atoms**. An element contains just one type of atom, and a compound contains two or more types of atom joined together. You cannot see atoms, even with a light microscope, because they are incredibly small. If you could line up oxygen atoms side by side along a fifteen-centimetre ruler, you would need one and a quarter billion of them!

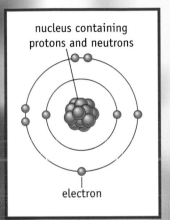

nucleus containing protons and neutrons

electron

◀ A model of an atom of oxygen. Every element has a different number of protons (atomic number). Each oxygen atom contains eight protons and eight neutrons. Its eight electrons are arranged in two energy levels or shells around the nucleus.

Atoms are made up of even smaller particles called **protons**, **neutrons** and **electrons**. There is a tiny **nucleus** at the centre of each atom that contains the protons and neutrons. The electrons are arranged in different energy levels, or shells, around the nucleus. The number of electrons in an atom and their arrangement around its nucleus are responsible for the reactions an element can make. However, most of an atom is empty space – if an atom were blown up to the same size as an Olympic running track, its nucleus would only be as big as a pea!

Elements and groups

Different elements react with other substances in different ways. When chemists first began to study chemical reactions this made it difficult for them to make sense of the reactions they observed. In 1869, a Russian chemist called Dimitri Mendeleev put each element into one of eight groups in a table. Each group contained elements with similar chemical properties. This made it much easier for chemists to work out what to expect when they reacted elements with each other. You can find the modern equivalent, the **periodic table**, on the next page.

CHAPTER 2

The periodic table, group 6 and oxygen

Chemists built on Mendeleev's work and eventually produced the modern **periodic table**, which you can see here. Each row in the table is called a **period**. The **elements** in a period are arranged in order of increasing **atomic number** (the atomic number is the number of **protons** in the **nucleus**). Each column in the table is called a **group**. The elements in each group have similar chemical properties to each other. For example, the elements in group 1 are very reactive, soft metals, and the elements in group 0 (zero) are very unreactive gases. The periodic table gets its name because these different chemical properties occur again regularly or periodically. The elements in each group also have the same number of electrons in their outer shell. The elements in group 6 all have six electrons in their outer shell.

▼ *This is the periodic table of the elements. Group 6 contains three non-metals: oxygen, sulphur, selenium.*

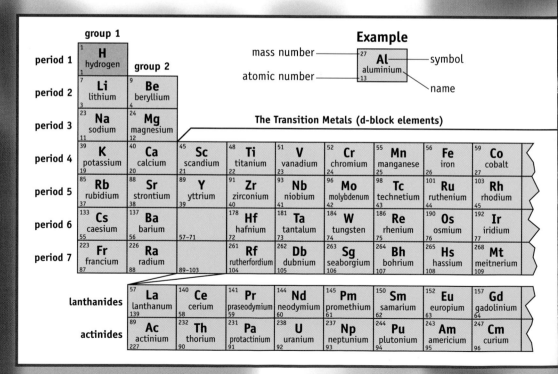

As you go down a group, the chemical properties of the elements change gradually. Oxygen, sulphur and selenium at the top of group 6 are all non-metals. Tellurium, in the middle of the group, is a metalloid, while polonium at the bottom is a metal. There is also an artificial element in group 6, below polonium. This element is temporarily called ununhexium (pronounced 'yoo-nun-hex-ee-um'), and very few **atoms** of it have been made. We do not know much about it because its atoms give off **radiation** and break down to form other elements within seconds of being made. However, chemists are certain that it is a metal because the element immediately above it in the group is a metal.

Group 6 and oxygen

In this book, you are going to find out all about oxygen, sulphur and the other elements in group 6, the compounds they make, and many of their uses.

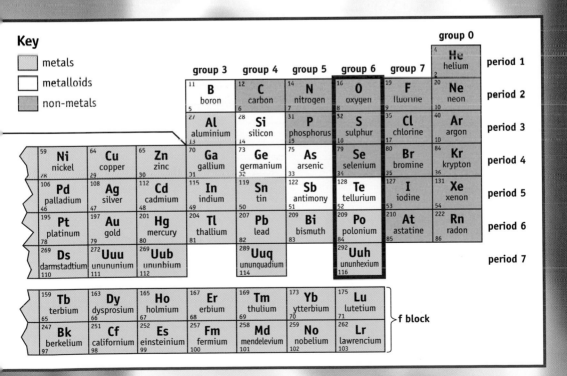

Elements of group 6

The **elements** in group 6 are sometimes called the chalcogens. There are six elements in the group: oxygen, sulphur, selenium, tellurium, polonium and ununhexium. Only one of them, oxygen, is a gas at room temperature – the rest are all solids. Oxygen, sulphur and selenium are non-metals, whilst polonium and ununhexium are metals. Tellurium is a metalloid, which means that its properties are between those of metals and non-metals.

16		
O		**oxygen**
	oxygen	*symbol: O • atomic number: 8 • non-metal*
8		

What does it look like? At room temperature, oxygen, O_2, is an odourless, tasteless and colourless gas. However, if it is cooled below $-183\,°C$, oxygen becomes a liquid with a slight blue colour. Almost every other element forms at least one **compound** with oxygen. Noble gases such as xenon are very unreactive, but even xenon reacts with oxygen. The name oxygen comes from Greek words meaning 'acid-former'. This is because when other non-metals react with oxygen, they form compounds that are acidic if dissolved in water.

Where is it found? Oxygen is the most common element in the Earth's crust, making up about 47 per cent of it. Oxygen also forms 21 per cent of the atmosphere.

What are its main uses? It is essential for the survival of almost all living things. Without it, animals and plants could not respire and so release energy from their food. Oxygen is also needed for things to burn – without it, you cannot start a fire or keep it going.

The word equation for respiration is:

glucose + oxygen → carbon dioxide + water

Liquid oxygen in store awaiting a launch at Kennedy Space Center. ▶

In a process called **photosynthesis**, plants use carbon dioxide, water and energy from light to make food. During photosynthesis, plants release oxygen into the atmosphere.

The word equation for photosynthesis is:

$$\text{carbon dioxide} + \text{water} \xrightarrow{\text{sunlight}} \text{glucose} + \text{oxygen}$$

32	**S**	**sulphur**
16	sulphur	*symbol: S • atomic number: 16 • non-metal*

What does it look like and where is it found? Sulphur can be found around volcanoes and has been known for thousands of years. It used to be called brimstone, and was said to be used by witches! Solid sulphur, S_8, has a light yellow colour and smells faintly of rotten eggs. It is hydrogen sulphide, H_2S, that has a strong rotten egg smell. Sulphur compounds are often found in natural **mineral** waters. Lead sulphide, PbS, is the natural mineral galena.

What are its main uses? When sulphur burns in air, it produces sulphur dioxide, SO_2, which can be used to preserve food. Fossil fuels such as coal and oil often contain sulphur. This means that when they burn, large quantities of sulphur dioxide escape into the atmosphere, where it reacts with water vapour to produce acid rain. This damages buildings and kills living things. The main use of sulphur is to make sulphuric acid, H_2SO_4, which can be used to manufacture **fertilizers** and explosives.

◀ *Volcanic sulphur mining deposits around a crater lake at Rawah Ijen volcano, Java, Indonesia. A sulphurous vent steams behind the man collecting sulphur.*

More elements of group 6

79	Se	selenium
34	selenium	symbol: Se • atomic number: 34 • non-metal

Where is it found? Selenium is only rarely found as the free **element**. There are few **minerals** containing selenium and it is normally extracted as a by-product from copper **refining**. The name selenium comes from the Greek word meaning 'Moon'.

What are its main uses? Selenium is an important trace mineral in a healthy diet. However, you do not need much of it and, like many substances needed by the body, it can also be poisonous in large amounts. The soil in some areas naturally contains large amounts of selenium, and grazing animals can be poisoned if they eat food from pastures growing there. Selenium is a **semi-conductor**, which means it can be used in computer chips.

128	Te	tellurium
52	tellurium	symbol: Te • atomic number: 52 • metalloid

Where is it found? There are few minerals containing tellurium, and it is normally extracted as a by-product from copper refining. The name tellurium comes from the Latin word meaning 'Earth'.

What does it look like? It is a shiny silvery-white solid, which is very **brittle** (it can be broken up very easily).

What are its main uses? Tellurium and its **compounds** are very poisonous. Even in tiny amounts, they can cause bad breath that smells like garlic, called 'tellurium breath'. Most of us are very unlikely to come into contact with a lot of tellurium, but where it is used in factories or laboratories it must be handled extremely carefully.

Tellurium is used in solar cells. These convert sunlight into electricity to power special cars like this one. ▶

Tellurium is also an important semi-conductor. It is used in solar cells (which convert light into electricity) and computer chips. It also improves the properties of steel and other metals, and it is used in detonators for explosives.

209 Po polonium 84	**polonium** symbol: Po • atomic number: 84 • metal

The famous scientists Marie and Pierre Curie discovered polonium in 1898. The name polonium comes from Poland, the country where Marie Curie was born.

What does it look like? Polonium is a **radioactive**, silvery metal, which is a solid at room temperature.

Where does it come from? It is extracted from an **ore** of uranium called pitchblende. It is incredibly rare – ten tonnes of pitchblende only contains about one thousandth of a gram of polonium!

What are its main uses? Polonium has very few commercial uses, but these include brushes that professional photographers use to remove dust from their films, and power sources for satellites.

292 Uuh ununhexium 116	**ununhexium** symbol: Uuh • atomic number: 116 • metal

Where is it found and what does it look like? Ununhexium (pronounced 'yoo-nun-hex-ee-um') was first made in 1999 at the Lawrence Berkeley National Laboratory in California. Other artificial metals have also been made there, including rutherfordium, dubnium and seaborgium. These new elements are made by bombarding metal targets with high-speed ions (**atoms** missing some **electrons**) in a machine called a particle accelerator. Ununhexium was made by smashing krypton ions into lead atoms. Very little is known about it because its atoms break apart to form other elements within milliseconds of being made. Ununhexium is a temporary name that means 'one-one-six'.

CHAPTER 3

Oxygen

Over 2000 years ago, the Greek philosophers, including Empedocles and Aristotle, believed that everything was made of just four **elements**. These were not the elements we know about today, but were earth, air, fire and water. Even though we now know that this idea was wrong, people thought so highly of Aristotle's writings that scientists only began to unravel the truth about 400 years ago.

In 1641, an English scientist called John Mayow experimented with air, live mice and burning candles. He discovered that the volume of air went down a bit when his mice were breathing it or when candles were burning in it. Mayow's experiments showed that air must contain at least two different gases. This meant that the ancient Greeks were wrong to think that air was an element.

A Swedish chemist called Carl Scheele did some more experiments on air in 1772. He also discovered that air contained at least two different gases. He called one of them 'foul air' because living things died in it and flames went out in it. We now know that 'foul air' is mostly nitrogen. Scheele called the other gas 'fire air', because living things and burning things needed it. This, of course, was oxygen. Scheele took so long to publish his results that two other scientists got the credit for discovering oxygen.

Joseph Priestley, an English clergyman with an interest in science, produced oxygen in 1774 by heating mercury oxide, HgO.

When mercury oxide is heated, it **decomposes** *(breaks down) to form mercury and oxygen:*

$$\text{mercury oxide} \xrightarrow{\text{heat}} \text{mercury} + \text{oxygen}$$

Priestley and two mice tried breathing in the new gas, and candle flames burnt extremely brightly in it. Later that year Priestley met Antoine Lavoisier, a French chemist. Lavoisier improved on Priestley's work and did many more experiments with the new gas. He also called it oxygen instead of 'fire air'.

Combustion

When fuels react with oxygen, they burn and release energy as heat and light. Burning is usually called **combustion** by chemists. Coal is largely made up of carbon which, when it burns, reacts with oxygen to produce carbon dioxide, CO_2. Oil and natural gas contain molecules called hydrocarbons. These are **compounds** of hydrogen and carbon. When hydrocarbons burn, the hydrogen in them reacts with oxygen to produce water, H_2O, and the carbon in them reacts with oxygen to produce carbon dioxide.

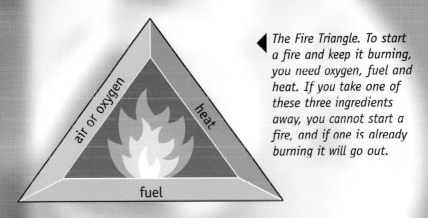

The Fire Triangle. To start a fire and keep it burning, you need oxygen, fuel and heat. If you take one of these three ingredients away, you cannot start a fire, and if one is already burning it will go out.

When coal burns, it produces carbon dioxide:

coal + oxygen → carbon dioxide

When oil and natural gas burn, they produce water and carbon dioxide:

hydrocarbon + oxygen → water + carbon dioxide

Respiration and combustion

Respiration is the chemical **reaction** that all the cells in our bodies use to release energy from food. Without it, we could not get the energy we need for all our body's processes, such as moving, growing and keeping warm. As the early scientists discovered, respiration and **combustion** are similar in many ways. Both reactions need oxygen, and both produce water and carbon dioxide. Both reactions are **oxidation** reactions, because oxygen is added during the reaction. They are also **exothermic** reactions, because they release energy.

The word equation for respiration is:

glucose + oxygen → carbon dioxide + water

Respiration happens in tiny objects in our cells called mitochondria.

However, respiration and combustion are not identical. We get the oxygen needed for respiration from the air that we breathe into our lungs. The oxygen passes into our blood where it joins on to a special molecule in our red blood cells, called haemoglobin. The blood carries the oxygen to our cells, and it also carries the waste carbon dioxide and water away from them. During combustion, energy is released very quickly but it is released only slowly by respiration. This is why we don't burst into flames because of respiration!

The Bunsen burner

Candle flames, and the safety flame from a Bunsen burner, are relatively cool flames that burn at about 680 °C. They burn slowly because the oxygen in the air has to diffuse or mix slowly with the burning fuel, which slows the reaction down. However, if the air hole in the Bunsen burner is opened, air is drawn into the chimney and mixes with the fuel there. This means that combustion can happen much faster, and as a result you see the familiar blue flame, which burns at about 1000 °C. If there is not enough oxygen for the reaction, we get incomplete combustion.

A Bunsen burner with its safety flame makes fairly cool (yellow) flames. If the air hole is opened, air mixes quickly with the gas and a very hot (blue) flame is made.

Carbon monoxide

Normally when a fuel such as natural gas burns, it produces water and carbon dioxide. However, if the supply of oxygen is reduced, incomplete combustion happens. Instead of reacting with oxygen, some of the carbon in the fuel is released as tiny carbon particles, which makes the flame smoky and sooty. Some of it also reacts with a little oxygen to produce carbon monoxide, CO, instead of carbon dioxide, CO_2.

Carbon monoxide is a colourless gas with no smell. It is also poisonous, and small amounts can make you fall asleep, while large amounts could kill you. Carbon monoxide joins on to the haemoglobin in your red blood cells more efficiently than oxygen, preventing your blood from carrying enough oxygen to your cells. Modern gas fires have plenty of ventilation built into them, and older homes usually have panels for ventilation in the walls, so you are unlikely to come across carbon monoxide. However, some people install carbon monoxide detectors in their homes as a precaution.

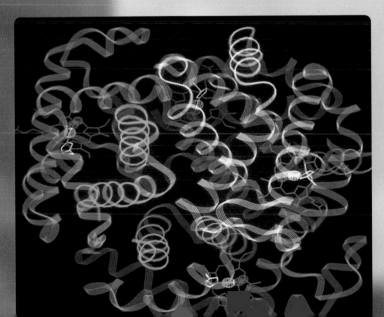

A computer graphic representation of a molecule of haemoglobin, a very large protein found in our red blood cells. Its job is to carry oxygen to the cells in our bodies.

Photosynthesis is the process plants use to make food using carbon dioxide, water and energy from light. During this process oxygen is released as a waste gas. Photosynthesis is very important for life on Earth because it produces the oxygen that living things need to respire. Even plants need to respire. During the day when there is a lot of sunlight, the rate of photosynthesis is more than the rate of **respiration**, and overall plants give out oxygen. Photosynthesis cannot happen in the dark, so at night plants actually take in oxygen overall. Plants produce far more oxygen during their lives than they use. There is also a vast amount of oxygen in the atmosphere, which means we will not run out!

The word equation for photosynthesis is:

$$\text{carbon dioxide + water} \xrightarrow{\text{sunlight}} \text{glucose + oxygen}$$

Photosynthesis happens in tiny green objects in plant cells called chloroplasts. Chloroplasts contain a protein called chlorophyll, which makes them green and absorbs light.

Plants need water and carbon dioxide for photosynthesis. They absorb water through their roots, and carbon dioxide from the air through their leaves. Farmers make sure their plants are watered regularly and, if they are growing their crop in greenhouses, they often add extra carbon dioxide to the air. This makes the plants grow faster because they can photosynthesize faster.

Evolution of the atmosphere

The modern atmosphere contains about 78 per cent nitrogen and 21 per cent oxygen. However, the original atmosphere four and a half billion years ago probably consisted mainly of carbon monoxide, carbon dioxide, water, methane and ammonia, but no oxygen. Scientists believe that they can explain the changes and that oxygen provides the key.

Energy from lightning and ultraviolet light broke up the water in the early atmosphere into its two **elements**, hydrogen and oxygen. About a billion years after the Earth formed, simple living things evolved and also released oxygen by photosynthesis. Just over two billion years ago, when there was about 0.2 per cent oxygen in the atmosphere, complex living things evolved. They were able to photosynthesize more efficiently than simple living things and released even more oxygen into the atmosphere. At first this oxygen reacted with any metals in the rocks as soon as it was produced. This process went on until about one billion years ago, when all the metals in the rocks that could react with oxygen had done so. It was after this that the levels of oxygen in the atmosphere began to increase rapidly, until the amount produced was balanced by the amount used for respiration and other processes.

As the levels of oxygen increased, the oxygen began to react with other gases in the atmosphere. It reacted with the carbon monoxide, CO, and the methane, CH_4, removing them totally from the atmosphere. The resulting carbon dioxide, CO_2, either dissolved in the oceans or was used up in photosynthesis. It reacted with ammonia, NH_3, to produce nitrogen, N_2. The levels of nitrogen were further increased as a result of the 'denitrifying' bacteria feeding on the ammonia.

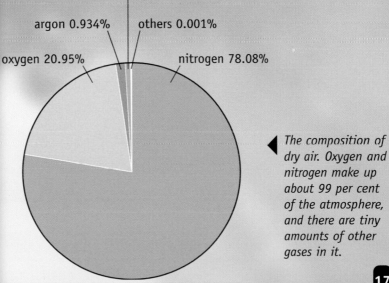

carbon dioxide 0.035%

argon 0.934%   others 0.001%

oxygen 20.95%   nitrogen 78.08%

The composition of dry air. Oxygen and nitrogen make up about 99 per cent of the atmosphere, and there are tiny amounts of other gases in it.

Ozone

Ozone, O_3, was discovered in 1840 by a German chemist called Christian Schönbein. Ozone molecules are made of three oxygen **atoms** joined together instead of the two atoms found in normal oxygen. Ozone is a pale blue gas, but it becomes a deep blue explosive liquid below −112 °C. Its name comes from the Greek word meaning 'to smell' because it has a sharp 'electrical' smell.

The ozone layer

When life first began on Earth, it was bombarded by ultraviolet light from the Sun. This killed living things by damaging the chemicals inside them. Seawater gives some protection from ultraviolet light, so for millions of years living things were found only in the sea.

When the amount of oxygen in the atmosphere increased because of **photosynthesis**, the ultraviolet light began to turn ordinary oxygen into ozone. This spread out and mixed with the other gases in the atmosphere. Eventually, about 90 per cent of the ozone became concentrated in the stratosphere, the part of the atmosphere between 10 km and 50 km above the Earth's surface. Scientists talk about an ozone layer, but we should remember that the ozone in the stratosphere is thinly mixed with other gases.

Once enough ozone formed, it shielded the surface of the Earth from ultraviolet light. This meant that about 400 million years ago, living things could start to live on the land, instead of just in the sea. Without the ozone layer, there would be no flowers or trees, the giant land dinosaurs would never have existed − and neither would we!

Holes in the ozone layer

Man-made chemicals called CFCs (chlorofluorocarbons) have been used since the 1920s for refrigerators, spray cans and dry cleaning. Ultraviolet light in the stratosphere breaks the CFCs down to produce very reactive particles called free radicals. These react with ozone and break it down faster than new ozone can form. As a result, there is now less ozone and less protection. Where there is very little ozone, particularly over the South Pole, 'holes' in the ozone layer occur. More ultraviolet light can reach the ground causing damage to vegetation, damage to eyes in animals and skin cancer. Most CFCs have been banned, but it will take many years for enough ozone to form to 'fill the holes' and repair the ozone layer.

Dangerous ozone

The ozone layer is good for us, but ozone at ground level is not. Although ozone can be used for food preservation and in disinfectants, it can cause stinging eyes and throats, breathing difficulties and headaches. It damages crops and materials such as plastics, rubber, paints and dyes. Laser printers and photocopiers produce ozone, so they need to be used in well-ventilated rooms. Sunlight causes the chemicals in vehicle exhaust fumes to react and produce ozone, which can be a big problem in cities during summer days. Ozone pollution can travel long distances from the cities and causes damage to forests and crops.

▼ *The Edwardians thought that ozone was good for them because it had an 'extra' oxygen atom. As rotting seaweed smells a little like ozone, they also thought that there was more ozone at the seaside, which gave them a good excuse to go on holiday there.*

Making oxygen

Oxygen in the air is produced by **photosynthesis**, but trying to cover millions of hectares of plants with plastic to capture oxygen for industrial use would be rather tricky. Luckily, there are lots of ways that chemists can produce oxygen. Some methods work well for making oxygen in the laboratory, and others are best on an industrial scale.

Oxygen in the laboratory

Oxygen was discovered by heating mercury oxide. Other **compounds** containing oxygen can also break down to release oxygen. One common way to produce oxygen in the laboratory is to heat solid potassium nitrate, KNO_3. This melts and breaks down to form bubbles of oxygen. It also forms liquid potassium nitrite, KNO_2, which turns solid again when cold.

Hydrogen peroxide, H_2O_2, is a chemical that slowly breaks down to make water and oxygen. But, if powdered manganese dioxide, MnO_2, is added to it, lots of bubbles of oxygen come out of it very quickly. This is because the manganese dioxide acts as a **catalyst**, which means that it can speed up this **reaction** without being used up.

Living things contain biological catalysts, called **enzymes**. Blood contains an enzyme called catalyse that does the same job as manganese dioxide. You can see the catalyst at work if you use hydrogen peroxide to clean out a graze or cut. The foam produced shows a rapid release of oxygen when the enzyme meets the hydrogen peroxdide.

When manganese dioxide powder is added to hydrogen peroxide solution, water and oxygen are produced. You can see the bubbles of oxygen rising through the liquid.

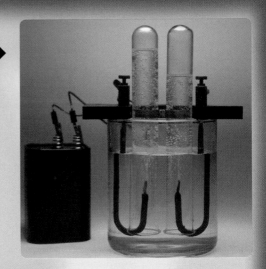

Water is a compound of two gases, hydrogen and oxygen. When electricity is passed through it, it breaks down to form hydrogen and oxygen. Bubbles of gas rise from the electrodes and collect in the test tubes.

Water is a compound of hydrogen and oxygen. If electricity is passed through it, especially if a little sulphuric acid has been added, water splits up into hydrogen and oxygen again. This process is called **electrolysis**, and you may see it done at school in a piece of apparatus called the Hofmann Voltammeter. Two metal **electrodes** carry the electricity into the water. Hydrogen bubbles come off at the negative electrode, and oxygen bubbles come off at the positive electrode. Electrolysis can be scaled up to make oxygen in industrial amounts but, as electricity is expensive, very little oxygen is made this way.

Industrial oxygen

At first, oxygen was made industrially using the Brin Process. This was named after Arthur and Leon Brin, the two brothers who developed it. Barium oxide, BaO, was heated in compressed air to make barium peroxide, BaO_2. When this was cooled and the pressure released, oxygen was given off and the barium peroxide turned back into barium oxide again. However, the modern method uses air in a very different way.

Most oxygen is now made from air by a process called **fractional distillation**. Oxygen made this way is more than 99.7 per cent pure. Air is chilled to remove any water vapour, and then it is cooled using powerful refrigerators. This causes the nitrogen and oxygen in the air to turn into liquids. The mixture of liquids is slowly warmed. The boiling point of nitrogen is -196 °C, so this turns back into a gas first and is removed. Oxygen boils off later at −183 °C, and is piped off and stored in pressurized cylinders.

Uses of oxygen

In 1825, Goldsworthy Gurney burnt hydrogen in a stream of oxygen gas, and aimed the hot flame at a piece of calcium oxide, CaO. It gave off light so bright, it could be seen many kilometres away! This sort of light was called limelight because calcium oxide is also called lime. Limelight was used to light theatre stages which is why we sometimes talk about people being 'in the limelight'. Although it has now gone out of fashion, limelight was the first commercial use of oxygen. Today, about five million tonnes of oxygen are now used every day for many other uses, including the manufacture of sulphuric acid and nitric acid, HNO_3.

Oxygen for respiration

The atmosphere becomes thinner as you go higher. As a result, mountain climbers can find it difficult to get enough oxygen when they breathe in. Airliners fly so high that there is too little oxygen in the air for passengers to breathe comfortably. The cabin is pressurized to keep the air inside close to normal atmospheric pressure, so everyone gets enough oxygen to breathe normally. If there is an emergency and the air pressure goes down, oxygen masks drop from the ceiling automatically.

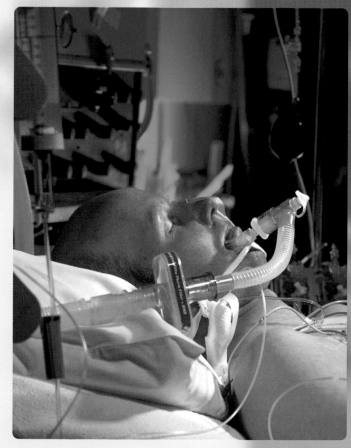

This man is a patient in the intensive care unit at hospital. The tube going into his mouth is part of the respirator that supplies him with oxygen.

In medicine, oxygen gas is used for life-support in emergencies, and it is also used as a carrier gas to help patients breathe in anaesthetic gas for operations. Divers need to carry their own supplies of oxygen underwater in metal gas tanks. Astronauts also need to take supplies of oxygen with them into space.

The Space Shuttle and the International Space Station use a mixture of 20 per cent oxygen and 80 per cent nitrogen at normal atmospheric pressure. The *Apollo* spacecraft, which took men to the Moon, had very thin walls to keep the mass low and so save on fuel. This meant that air at normal atmospheric pressure could not be used inside. To make sure that the astronauts had enough oxygen to breathe without bursting the walls of their spacecraft, pure oxygen at low pressure was used. This is not without danger – pure oxygen allows things to burn very quickly, and three astronauts were killed in a fire that raged through *Apollo 1* during a ground test in 1967.

Oxygen in industry

Metals such as steel are cut using an oxy-acetylene torch. A flammable gas called acetylene (ethyne, C_2H_2), is burnt in a stream of oxygen to produce a flame at about 3000 °C. The steel is heated using the oxy-acetylene torch, and a stream of oxygen gas is run over it. This causes the steel to oxidize and crumble away.

Oxygen is used to reduce the amount of impurities in steel, such as carbon. Freshly made iron contains about 4 per cent carbon, which makes it hard but **brittle**. Oxygen is blown into liquid iron, where it reacts with the carbon. This escapes as carbon monoxide and carbon dioxide, and the carbon content is lowered to less than 1 per cent. The steel that is formed is **malleable**.

Oxidation and rusting

Oxidation reactions happen when a substance reacts with oxygen (becomes oxidized). They are very common and some oxidation reactions, such as iron rusting and food going off, cause us problems.

Rusting

Iron reacts with water and oxygen to form hydrated iron oxide, $Fe_2O_3.H_2O$. This is the familiar brown rust you get if you leave iron or steel objects out in the rain. Rust can weaken bridges, buildings and vehicles, and it stops machinery working smoothly. If water and oxygen (from the air), or both, are kept away from iron and steel, rusting can be stopped. Air can be kept away by oiling, painting or coating the metal in plastic. However, once an object has started to rust there is no point in just painting over the rust. The rust will simply flake off, taking the paint away and exposing fresh metal to the air and water. Sensitive computer components cannot be oiled or painted but can be stored vacuum-packed in plastic, which keeps the air out.

▼ *The Forth Rail Bridge crosses the estuary of the River Forth in Scotland. It contains 55,000 tonnes of steel and is covered with over half a square kilometre of paint to stop it rusting. Keeping it painted is a full-time job.*

In food cans, a thin layer of tin (which does not react easily with oxygen) is coated over steel. Steel coated with a thin layer of zinc is called galvanized steel, and is often used to make cars. Zinc is more reactive than iron, so the zinc reacts with oxygen first. This is called **sacrificial protection**.

Aluminium is a reactive metal that reacts with oxygen to form aluminium oxide, Al_2O_3. This forms a thin, but tough, layer on the surface of the aluminium. Unlike rust, it does not flake off, and keeps air and water away from the metal beneath. Aluminium can be used outside for doors and window frames. Stainless steel is an alloy of iron and chromium, which is used for cutlery. It does not rust because a tough, invisible surface layer of chromium oxide, Cr_2O_3, resists rusting forms.

If an unreactive metal, such as gold, is chosen for a particular job it also avoids the problems created by rust. Gold is quite soft and very expensive, so it is only used where small amounts are needed, such as the edge-connectors in computer chips.

Food and antioxidants

Vegetables and fruit, such as potatoes and apples, turn brown when they are peeled, and food gradually goes off as it is stored. One of the reasons for this is that the substances inside food react with oxygen in the air. Fats and oils, for example, become unpleasant with rancid tastes and smells once they react with oxygen.

Manufacturers sometimes add chemicals to food to prevent or slow down the oxidation reactions and make the food last longer. These chemicals are called **antioxidants**. Some foods contain their own natural antioxidants, such as vitamin C and vitamin E. The oxidation reactions can also be slowed down by keeping air away, so food may be preserved by sealing it in a vacuum or in a special atmosphere containing only a little oxygen.

Metal extraction

A few metals do not react with oxygen and can be found in their native state as metal mixed with rock. Gold and platinum are found as free metals, which can be separated from the rock around them. Most metals, such as iron and aluminium, do react with oxygen and are found as metal oxides. The metal oxides are called **minerals**, and most minerals are mixed with other substances such as sand, silicon dioxide, SiO_2, to form **ores**. To get the metal out of an ore, the oxygen must be removed from it.

Iron and the blast furnace

Haematite is an iron ore that contains iron oxide. Iron can be produced from iron ore relatively cheaply using a blast furnace. This is a giant metal tube about 90 m high, lined with heat-resistant material. Blasts of hot air are blown in at the bottom to supply the oxygen needed for the **reactions** inside. The raw materials needed to make iron (iron ore, limestone and coke) are dropped in from the top.

Coke is mostly carbon, and is made by **roasting** coal. It reacts with the oxygen in the blast furnace to produce carbon monoxide gas. This reacts with the iron ore to produce iron and carbon dioxide.

The word equation for producing iron from iron oxide in the blast furnace is:

$$\text{iron oxide} + \text{carbon monoxide} \xrightarrow{\text{heat}} \text{iron} + \text{carbon dioxide}$$

Removing oxygen from an oxide is called **reduction**. *In this reaction, carbon monoxide reduces the iron oxide.*

The liquid iron that is produced contains sandy impurities. These are removed using the limestone. Calcium oxide from the limestone reacts with the impurities to make slag, which floats on the surface of the liquid iron. The slag is easily removed, to leave purified iron behind.

▲ *A steel worker taking a sample from a blast furnace. One of the processes needed to convert iron into steel involves a stream of oxygen gas that reacts with carbon impurities in iron and removes them.*

Iron straight from the blast furnace contains about 4 per cent carbon and is called pig iron. Steel be produced from the iron by lowering its carbon content using oxygen gas.

Aluminium

Bauxite is an aluminium ore that contains aluminium oxide. Aluminium is much more reactive than iron, which means that oxygen cannot be removed from its ore simply by heating it with carbon monoxide. Instead, electricity is used to break down the aluminium oxide into aluminium and oxygen.

Purified aluminium oxide, called alumina, is melted and powerful electric currents are sent through it. This causes the aluminium and oxygen to separate in a process called **electrolysis**. The liquid aluminium is tapped off and solidified in moulds. Meanwhile, the oxygen bubbles out of the liquid alumina and some of it reacts with the blocks of carbon that carry the electricity. This causes them to burn away and they have to be replaced every two weeks. As electricity is expensive, aluminium costs more than iron, even though there is more of it in the Earth's crust.

Water

Water is a **compound** of hydrogen and oxygen. It is the most abundant compound on Earth and covers about 71 per cent of the Earth's surface. There are about 1,400,000,000 cubic kilometres of water, of which 97 per cent is seawater! Water forms about 60 per cent of our body mass and we can survive only a few days without it. In 1784, Henry Cavendish showed that water is made when hydrogen and oxygen react together. In 1800, within months of the invention of the electric battery, William Nicholson discovered that water could be separated into hydrogen and oxygen when electricity is passed through it. Both these discoveries have led to important uses in the modern world.

Electrolysis of water

Some compounds break down into simpler substances when electricity is passed through them. This is called **electrolysis**. Two electrodes are used to conduct the electricity into the compound. If electricity is passed through slightly acidified water using platinum electrodes, the water breaks down into its two **elements**, hydrogen and oxygen. Electrolysis is used to produce oxygen in the laboratory, but it would cost too much to produce a lot of industrial oxygen this way. However, there is one place where a lot of water and electricity are found together – in a nuclear submarine!

Nuclear submarines can stay underwater for up to six months at a time. They are limited only by the amount of food that can be carried to feed the crew. Nuclear reactors produce large amounts of heat from small amounts of nuclear fuel. This heat is used to boil water to produce steam, which turns electricity generators. The electricity powers the submarine and is used to make oxygen from seawater for the submariners to breathe.

A nuclear-powered submarine. ▶
Electricity from the nuclear reactor is used to split seawater into hydrogen and oxygen.

▲ In the International Space Station, hydrogen and oxygen react together in fuel cells to make electricity and drinking water for the astronauts on board.

The hydrogen fuel cell

In 1842, Sir William Grove found that electricity was produced if two platinum strips were half covered with sulphuric acid, and hydrogen was passed over one strip and oxygen over the other. This was electrolysis in reverse – instead of using electricity to split water into hydrogen and oxygen, he discovered that electricity can be made if hydrogen and oxygen react together to make water. Grove's 'gas battery' has been improved a lot over the years, and the modern fuel cell is beginning to find many uses.

The only waste product from a hydrogen fuel cell is water, which makes it very attractive as an environmentally friendly power source for vehicles. The Space Shuttle and the International Space Station use fuel cells to make electricity from hydrogen and oxygen, and drinking water is a useful by-product for the astronauts. There is only one problem that stops fuel cells from being more widely used – hydrogen is a highly explosive gas, and needs careful storage and handling. In addition, the processes needed to produce it from other chemicals may cause pollution.

Carbon dioxide

Water is a liquid at room temperature and most of the remaining oxides are solids. However, a few such as sulphur dioxide and carbon dioxide, are gases. Laughing gas, which is nitrous oxide, N_2O, is used by some dentists as an anaesthetic, but carbon dioxide is probably the most familiar gaseous oxide.

Fermentation

Carbon dioxide is one of the **products** of **fermentation** by yeast. Yeast are microscopic single-celled fungi, and they contain **enzymes** that can break down sugar to release energy, carbon dioxide and ethanol (alcohol).

The word equation for fermentation is:

$$\text{glucose} \xrightarrow{\text{enzymes in yeast}} \text{carbon dioxide} + \text{ethanol}$$

Yeasts are used in bread making because the carbon dioxide they release makes the dough rise. They are also used in wine and beer making because they release ethanol.

The greenhouse effect

Carbon dioxide is given off when wood and **fossil fuels** burn. It is very good at absorbing infrared **radiation**, so it traps heat in the atmosphere. This is called the greenhouse effect because the carbon dioxide keeps in heat like the glass in a greenhouse, keeping the Earth's surface at an average temperature of 14 °C. Without it, the average surface temperature of our planet would be −18 °C, almost as cold as the Moon.

People are burning increasing amounts of fossil fuel, so more carbon dioxide is being released into the atmosphere than can be removed naturally. As the level of carbon dioxide has gone up, so has the average temperature at the Earth's surface. This is called global warming, and is leading to changing weather patterns. The polar ice caps may melt causing sea levels to rise, flooding lowland areas.

▲ *Solid carbon dioxide, called 'dry ice', is used for special effects. It produces the thick white fog often seen at rock concerts, like this one.*

Frozen food and foggy films

If carbon dioxide is frozen it makes 'dry ice'. This has a surface temperature of −78.5 °C, so it is used to keep food and medical samples cold while they are transported. Solid carbon dioxide is a very unusual substance because it sublimes when it warms up. This means that it turns into a gas without becoming a liquid. When dry ice warms up, it sublimes and creates a white mist. This is the white mist that is used for special effects in films and rock concerts.

Fire extinguishers and fizzy drinks

Carbon dioxide does not allow fuels to burn, so it is used in fire extinguishers. When the fire extinguisher is used, very cold carbon dioxide comes out. This removes heat and oxygen from the fire, and helps to put it out. Carbon dioxide is the gas that makes drinks fizzy. The gas is added to the drink under pressure so that more dissolves in the liquid than could happen at normal atmospheric pressure. When the drink is opened, the pressure is released and lots of bubbles of carbon dioxide are produced as a result.

A lot of substances contain oxygen. Some of these substances give up their oxygen very easily, which makes things burn.

Gunpowder

More than one thousand years ago, the Chinese found that a mixture of carbon, sulphur and potassium nitrate would burn violently if set on fire. They had discovered gunpowder. The potassium nitrate, KNO_3, provides the oxygen needed for the mixture to burn, so it is called an oxidant. When gunpowder burns, lots of hot gases are produced. If the gunpowder is burnt in a container, it is difficult for these gases to escape and pressure builds up inside until it explodes. The discovery of gunpowder led to the invention of bombs, bullets and fireworks. The oxidant in fireworks is usually potassium chlorate, $KClO_3$.

Every 5 November, fireworks like these celebrate the foiling of the Gunpowder Plot. On this day in 1605, Guy Fawkes was caught with 36 barrels of gunpowder under the House of Lords, in an attempt to blow up the King and the Houses of Parliament.

Rocket fuel

Rocket scientists can use oxidants too, but they choose ones that launch their rockets into space, rather than ones that explode! Modern solid rocket fuels use oxidants such as ammonium perchlorate, NH_4ClO_4, rather than potassium nitrate. Solid rocket motors are used to launch satellites, but the largest ones ever made are those used to help launch the Space Shuttle. Each booster contains 500 tonnes of fuel! The speed of the burn is controlled by the shape of the boosters, which are tall and thin, and by metal plates inside them. Once they have been ignited, they only shut down when all the fuel has gone.

Rocks not rockets

Some substances, such as calcium carbonate, $CaCO_3$, contain a lot of oxygen but do not give it up easily at all. This means that they cannot help things to burn. However, they often make good building materials. Marble, chalk and limestone are all forms of nearly pure calcium carbonate.

Marble is a hard rock that can be polished to an attractive, shiny finish. It is used for statues, kitchen and bathroom surfaces and as a cladding on buildings. Limestone is a tough rock used to construct roads and buildings. Chalk is a white crumbly rock that can be used to make cement. This is made by heating a mixture of chalk and clay together. Concrete is a mixture of sand, aggregate (small stones) and cement. About five billion tonnes of concrete are now used in the world each year!

If calcium carbonate is heated, it **decomposes** to form calcium oxide and carbon dioxide. Calcium oxide is a base, which means it can react with acids to **neutralize** them. Most soils are naturally slightly acidic, but they can become more acidic when artificial fertilizers are added to them. Crops do not grow well if the soil becomes too acidic, so farmers may apply powdered calcium oxide to their fields. Once this is ploughed in, it neutralizes some of the acid in the soils, which helps the crops to grow better.

Oxygen in complex molecules

Living things produce very large and complex molecules by joining lots of small molecules together. These molecules contain oxygen, and oxygen **atoms** are involved in joining them together.

Sweet and tough

Sugars are called carbohydrates because they contain carbon, hydrogen and oxygen. Two molecules of a simple sugar can join together to make more complex sugars. For example, glucose and fructose join together to make sucrose, which is cane sugar. When glucose and galactose join together they make lactose, which is found in milk. If thousands of glucose molecules join together, they make very large molecules such as starch, which is found in bread and rice. If the glucose molecules join together in a different way, they make cellulose, which is the tough molecule found in plant cell walls.

Proteins

Proteins are large molecules made from smaller molecules called amino acids. Many different proteins exist and all do different jobs. However, they are all made from about twenty different amino acids. Amino acids contain oxygen, and they join on to each other using a type of chemical bond called a peptide bond. In this bond, a nitrogen atom works like a bridge joining the amino acids together, but an oxygen atom is an important part of this bridge.

▼ *The ester bond and the peptide (amide) bond.*

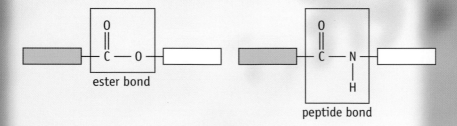

Fats, oil and DNA

Fats and oils are made from two different molecules, both of which contain oxygen. These are fatty acids and glycerol (a type of complex alcohol). Up to three fatty acid molecules can join on to a glycerol molecule using chemical **bonds** called ester bonds. In each ester bond, an oxygen atom works like a bridge that joins the two smaller molecules together.

DNA stands for deoxyribonucleic acid, which is a long name and often a very long molecule. A single DNA molecule can be 7 cm long, and human cells contain 2 m of it! DNA contains the genetic code for producing the proteins a cell needs. It is made from smaller molecules called nucleotides, and each nucleotide contains one of four different substances called bases. The different nucleotides are joined together in countless combinations using ester bonds.

Artificial polymers

Chemists have learnt how to join lots of small molecules together to produce very big molecules, called **polymers**. They can make polymers from lots of molecules joined end to end using ester bonds. These polymers are called polyesters because they contain lots of ester bonds. Polyester fibres, such as Terylene®, are used to make soft and hardwearing clothes. Polyester can also be used to make bottles, smartcards and videotape.

Chemists can also make polymers containing amide bonds. These bonds are identical to the peptide bonds found in proteins, but have a different name. The polymers are called polyamides because they contain lots of amide bonds. Polyamides, such as Nylon®, are used to make ropes, shirts and tights.

◀ *Polyester is so versatile that it can be made into soft or hard materials. These smartcards are made of polyester.*

CHAPTER 4

Sulphur

Many **minerals** contain sulphur. It is also found as the free **element** and has been known for thousands of years. The Romans used sulphur as a disinfectant, but today it has many uses including making drugs, dyes, **fungicides**, **insecticides**, matches and sulphuric acid. Sulphur is needed to make rubber tough enough for tyres in a process called vulcanization. World production of sulphur is over 58 million tonnes per year!

Manufacture of sulphur from sulphides

Metals are often found as sulphur **compounds** called sulphides. Minerals containing sulphur include galena (lead sulphide), pyrite (iron sulphide), sphalerite (zinc sulphide) and cinnabar (mercury sulphide). Liquid sulphur is produced if these minerals are **roasted** (heated strongly for a long time). About 15 per cent of the sulphur produced is made by roasting metal sulphides.

Sulphur the element

Sulphur is found as the free element near volcanoes and hot springs. It exists in three common forms, called **allotropes**. Plastic sulphur forms when molten sulphur is cooled rapidly by pouring it into cold water. It is a tough, elastic substance, which can be bent and twisted until it turns into one of the crystalline forms. Rhombic sulphur and monoclinic sulphur are both yellow crystalline solids. They consist of molecules with rings of eight sulphur **atoms**. However, the molecules are arranged differently in the two different crystals.

The Frasch Process

Until about a hundred years ago, most sulphur was produced from volcanic deposits and mines in Sicily. Other deposits are found in North America, China, Japan and Poland, but can be up to 900 m below the surface. The Frasch Process, invented in 1891 by an American chemical engineer, uses superheated water to mine sulphur from deep underground. Three steel tubes, one inside the other, are driven underground to reach the sulphur deposits.

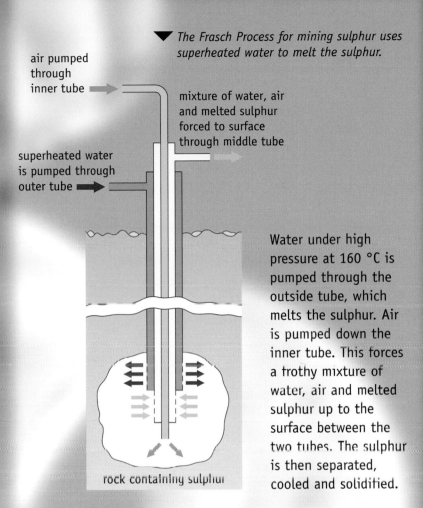

The Frasch Process for mining sulphur uses superheated water to melt the sulphur.

air pumped through inner tube →

mixture of water, air and melted sulphur forced to surface through middle tube →

superheated water is pumped through outer tube →

rock containing sulphur

Water under high pressure at 160 °C is pumped through the outside tube, which melts the sulphur. Air is pumped down the inner tube. This forces a frothy mixture of water, air and melted sulphur up to the surface between the two tubes. The sulphur is then separated, cooled and solidified.

The Claus Process

The Frasch Process is still used widely, but now more than half our sulphur is produced in a different way. Hydrogen sulphide, H_2S, is a very smelly and highly poisonous gas. Natural gas that contains hydrogen sulphide is called 'sour' because of the smell. Crude oil often contains sulphur compounds, and hydrogen sulphide is made when crude oil is processed in oil refineries. When fuels containing hydrogen sulphide are burnt, they make gases that cause acid rain. The Claus Process, invented by an English chemical engineer in 1883, produces sulphur from hydrogen sulphide. As a result, a highly unpleasant substance is converted into sulphur, which is a useful substance. It has the added attraction of producing environmentally friendly 'low-sulphur' fuels, which produce less acid rain.

Fools, boiled eggs and spa water

Sulphur **compounds** are often very unpleasant. In particular, hydrogen sulphide has an offensive smell similar to rotten eggs, and sulphur dioxide makes our eyes sting. On the other hand, iron sulphide has earned the name 'fools gold' because it is a shiny yellow **ore** that looks like gold.

Fool's gold

Pyrite is a compound of iron and sulphur, called iron sulphide, FeS. It is a shiny yellow solid, similar to gold. In the 1849 California Gold Rush, lots of would-be miners went to California hoping to become rich by finding gold. Sadly, the only thing that many of them found was pyrite. Pyrite is far less valuable than gold but looks similar and can be used in costume jewellery. It is also a valuable ore that can be **roasted** to produce iron and sulphur.

Boiled eggs

You may have noticed that the yolks of hard-boiled eggs often have a ring of blue-green colour round their edges. This is caused by iron sulphide, which forms naturally when the egg is boiled. A protein in the egg yolk contains iron, which is released when the egg is cooked. Tiny amounts of hydrogen sulphide are released from proteins in the egg white at the same time. When the iron from the yolk meets the hydrogen sulphide from the white, iron sulphide is formed, causing the coloured ring.

If you have ever smelt a hard-boiled egg or a rotten egg, you will know what hydrogen sulphide smells like. Hydrogen sulphide is a smelly gas that is poisonous in large amounts. It can bring on asthma attacks, yet some people go out of their way to drink and bathe in water that contains it because of the water's reputation as a medicinal cure.

An iron sulphide ring around the yolk in a hard-boiled egg. Soft-boiled eggs do not have this ring because they are not cooked for long enough to release the iron and hydrogen sulphide.

▲ *Harrogate in the north of England is famous for its mineral waters. The Royal Pump Room is built over four wells and visitors can sample the sulphur water. If you can manage to forget the smell of rotten eggs, the water just tastes salty.*

Spa water

If you are unlucky, your hot water supply can smell bad. Hot water heaters often contain a magnesium rod to protect the heater from corroding. However, this can react with sulphate salts in the water to produce hydrogen sulphide. The gas is corrosive and will damage iron and steel, and even concrete.

Some natural **mineral** waters contain dissolved hydrogen sulphide. People have valued these waters for medical uses for thousands of years, in spite of their smell (or possibly because of it). Mineral water containing sulphur compounds is supposed to be good for your liver. It is sometimes called hepatic water, after the Greek word for liver. Spa towns give visitors the chance to bathe in the water to help cure skin diseases. They can also drink the water, which they believe will help to cure all sorts of problems, including constipation and flatulence.

Sulphur dioxide

Sulphur burns with a blue flame and produces a choking gas that makes white fumes in air. This gas is sulphur dioxide, SO_2. It causes stinging eyes and breathing problems, particularly in people with asthma. Volcanic gases contain sulphur dioxide, but extra amounts are released into the atmosphere when natural gas, oil and coal are burnt.

Uses of sulphur dioxide

Sulphur dioxide dissolves easily in water to make sulphurous acid, H_2SO_3, which can be used for bleaches and disinfectants. It can be used to make chemicals called sulphites, which are used to preserve food such as sausages. Sodium sulphite, Na_2SO_3, is used to make sodium thiosulphate, $Na_2S_2O_3$. Sodium thiosulphate is sometimes called 'hypo', and photographers use it to 'fix' their photographs.

▼ These foods have been preserved using sulphur dioxide. Dried fruit and vegetables are often preserved by this method.

Sulphur dioxide is a very useful food preservative. It makes acidic conditions in the food that micro-organisms cannot easily survive. Dried fruit and soft drinks are often preserved using sulphur dioxide. Only very small amounts are used, so you are unlikely to smell or taste it. Sulphur dioxide is also used to bleach wool, straw and paper.

Acid rain

Rain is naturally slightly acidic because it contains dissolved carbon dioxide, which produces a weak acid called carbonic acid, H_2CO_3. This is not a problem because natural bases in the rivers, lakes and soil **neutralize** the acid. These include the calcium carbonate in rocks such as limestone. This reacts with the acid to produce calcium hydrogencarbonate, $Ca(HCO_3)_2$, which dissolves in the water. However, because of human activities, the rain in many parts of the world has become more acidic than natural processes can neutralize.

Large amounts of sulphur dioxide are released from vehicles using petrol and diesel that contains sulphur compounds, from coal-fired power stations, and from metal smelters that use metal sulphide **ores**. It reacts with oxygen in the air and water in the clouds to produce sulphuric acid. This acid causes the rain to become very acidic. In places, it can be as strong as lemon juice or vinegar! As a result, rocks and soil become weathered very quickly. Forests and crops are damaged, and rivers and lakes become so acidic that almost everything in them dies. Buildings and bridges are damaged by acid rain because it reacts with metal and stone.

Beating acid rain

The acid from the rain can be neutralized by adding chemicals such as lime to fields and lakes, but this does not stop more acid rain falling. A better way to beat acid rain is to reduce the amount of sulphur dioxide escaping in the first place. In power stations, this can be achieved by reacting the sulphur dioxide with powdered limestone to make calcium sulphate, $CaSO_4$. We can all play a part if we use low sulphur fuels and use less fuel. We can do this by walking or cycling instead of going by car, and by using less electricity.

Sulphuric acid

The main use of sulphur dioxide is to make sulphuric acid. More sulphuric acid is produced in the world than any other chemical – about 150 million tonnes each year! Most of this sulphuric acid goes to make **fertilizers**, but it has many other uses including plastics, paints and explosives.

▼ *Sugar is a molecule containing carbon, hydrogen and oxygen* **atoms.** *When concentrated sulphuric acid is added to it, a hot, steamy column of carbon like this forms. The acid reacts with the sugar molecules, removing the hydrogen and oxygen atoms as water, and leaving carbon behind.*

The Contact Process

Nearly all sulphuric acid is produced using the Contact Process. It is called this because sulphur dioxide and oxygen react together in contact with the surface of a **catalyst**. There are three main stages. The first stage is to produce sulphur dioxide by burning sulphur in air.

The word equation for the first stage of the Contact Process is:

sulphur + oxygen → sulphur dioxide

The next stage is to react the sulphur dioxide with oxygen from the air to make a gas called sulphur trioxide, SO_3. This would be a slow **reaction** normally, so a catalyst is used to speed it up. The catalyst is a solid metal oxide called vanadium(V) oxide, sometimes called vanadium pentoxide, V_2O_5. Sulphur dioxide molecules and oxygen molecules can get close together on its surface and react with each other. A temperature of 450 °C and a pressure of twice normal atmospheric pressure is needed to get a really good rate of reaction.

The word equation for the second stage is:

$$\text{sulphur dioxide} + \text{oxygen} \xrightarrow{\text{vanadium(V) oxide}} \text{sulphur trioxide}$$

The vanadium(V) oxide is a catalyst for this reaction.
This means it speeds up the reaction without getting used up.

The third stage is to react the sulphur trioxide with water to make sulphuric acid, H_2SO_4.

The overall word equation for the third stage of the Contact Process is:

$$\text{sulphur trioxide} + \text{water} \rightarrow \text{sulphuric acid}$$

However, the two chemicals cannot be just mixed together because they react violently with each other. Instead, the sulphur trioxide is mixed with concentrated (98 per cent) sulphuric acid to form an even more concentrated sulphuric acid called oleum. This is an oily liquid that makes lots of fumes if it is exposed to the air. The oleum is diluted with water back to 98 per cent sulphuric acid. Some of this is recycled to react with more sulphur trioxide, and the rest is stored ready to sell to customers. Overall, the sulphur trioxide has reacted with water.

Uses of sulphuric acid

Pure sulphuric acid is a colourless oily liquid that does not smell. The acid that is sold as 'concentrated' sulphuric acid is 98.3 per cent sulphuric acid. When it is added to water, a tremendous amount of heat is released – often enough to boil the mixture! Chemists always remember to add the acid slowly to cold water if they want to dilute it, rather than adding water to the acid. Sulphuric acid is corrosive. This means that it will damage skin, clothes, metals and other materials, and it must be handled with great care. Sulphuric acid is used in car batteries, but most of it is used to make other substances, rather than being used directly.

Car batteries

The most widely used car battery is called the lead-acid accumulator, invented by Gaston Planté in 1860. Lead-acid accumulators contain plates made of lead and lead oxide, PbO, and they are filled with 33 per cent sulphuric acid. When the battery is used, lead sulphate, $PbSO_4$, forms at the **electrodes** and water builds up in the acid. Drivers can check the battery condition by measuring the density of the acid. This is about 1.28 g/cm^3 in a fully charged battery, but it falls as water builds up in the acid. When the density gets to about 1.12 g/cm^3 the battery is flat and needs recharging. It is recharged by passing electricity into it, which causes the sulphuric acid, lead and lead oxide to form again.

Sulphates

Dilute sulphuric acid reacts with metals and bases to produce salts called sulphates, which are very useful materials. Copper sulphate, $CuSO_4$, is used in dyeing and printing calico cloth. Zinc sulphate, $ZnSO_4$, is used as an antiseptic, and iron sulphate, $FeSO_4$, is used for making ink and as a medicine. Magnesium sulphate, $MgSO_4$, is often called Epsom Salt. It gets its name from the **mineral** water at Epsom in England, which contains magnesium sulphate. Epsom Salt is manufactured by reacting sulphuric acid with a mineral called magnesite, which contains magnesium carbonate, $MgCO_3$. Epsom Salt has many uses, including cosmetic lotions, bath salts, laxatives, **fertilizers**, fireproofing and the 'snow' in films.

Calcium sulphate, $CaSO_4$, is found in a sedimentary rock called gypsum. It can also be made when sulphur dioxide is scrubbed from the waste gases of coal-fired power stations. Gypsum is used for plaster and plasterboard to line walls and ceilings in buildings. Natural gypsum contains water chemically bonded to the calcium sulphate crystals. If gypsum is heated to 100 °C, the water is removed to leave plaster of Paris behind. Plaster of Paris (named after the large deposits of gypsum near Paris) expands slightly when water is added to it, then sets hard. This means it can be used to make casts that hold broken bones still while they mend.

◀ *Gypsum is mainly made up of calcium sulphate and has many uses in the building trade. A plasterer is using it here to line the walls and ceilings of this building.*

More uses of sulphuric acid

Plants need **minerals**, especially nitrogen, phosphorus and potassium, to grow properly. Farmers and gardeners may add artificial **fertilizers** to the soil to provide the minerals plants need. Sulphuric acid is vital to the production of some of these fertilizers, and this is its biggest single use.

Fertilizers

Calcium phosphate, $Ca_3(PO_4)_2$, is found in rock phosphate, and would make a good source of phosphorus for plants except for one drawback. Unfortunately, it does not dissolve in water, so plants cannot take it up through their roots. To get around the problem, fertilizer manufacturers turn it into ammonium phosphate, which does dissolve in water. They do this in two steps.

In the first step, the calcium phosphate is reacted with concentrated sulphuric acid to make phosphoric acid and calcium sulphate. The calcium sulphate, of course, is gypsum. This can be filtered off and processed to make plasterboard.

In the second step, the phosphoric acid, H_3PO_4, is reacted with ammonia, NH_3, to make ammonium phosphate, $(NH_4)_3PO_4$. Plants are able to take this up through their roots, and it supplies nitrogen and phosphorus. In this way, sulphuric acid is vital in the conversion of calcium phosphate into useful fertilizer. Another useful fertilizer can be made by reacting ammonia and sulphuric acid together. This produces ammonium sulphate, which also dissolves in water and provides plants with nitrogen.

Detergents, washing powders and drugs

Sodium dodecyl sulphate is a synthetic (man-made) detergent made by reacting sulphuric acid with chemicals made from crude oil. Sodium dodecyl sulphate is found in many products, including shower gels and toothpaste. Synthetic detergents have many advantages over soap, which is made by heating vegetable oils with alkalis such as sodium hydroxide. They dissolve better in water, they form lather even in hard water areas, and they can be made from

▲ Different artificial fertilizers are tested in nitrogen
input trials, comparing a plot treated with normal
levels of nitrogen application and crops with none.
Without fertilizer, crops grow very poorly.

by-products of oil **refining** instead of from vegetable oils.
Washing powders are a combination of detergents, soaps and
other chemicals including sodium sulphate (which helps to
keep the powder dry). The chemical process in which
sulphuric acid is used to make detergents is called
sulphonation, which is an important step in the manufacture
of many pharmaceuticals.

Explosives
Christian Schönbein, the chemist who discovered ozone,
invented an explosive by accident in 1845. He spilled a
mixture of acids that included sulphuric acid, and wiped
them up with his wife's cotton apron. The acids reacted with
the cotton to form an explosive called guncotton, and the
apron later exploded! Nitroglycerine is another powerful
explosive that needs sulphuric acid for its manufacture, and
from this many other explosives can be made. These include
dynamite, invented in 1866 by Alfred Nobel after a
nitroglycerine explosion blew up his factory and killed five
men, including his brother. Nobel died in 1896, and left
money in his will to start the Nobel Prizes, which were first
awarded in 1901.

CHAPTER 5

Selenium

Selenium was discovered in 1817 by the Swedish chemist, Jöns Berzelius, who found what he thought was tellurium in sulphuric acid from a factory. He discovered later that it was a new **element** with very similar properties to tellurium (see page 52). Tellurium is named after the Latin word for Earth, and Berzelius called the new element selenium, after the Greek word for Moon.

Properties of selenium

There are several common **allotropes** or forms of selenium. Allotropes are forms of an element that look different from each other because their **atoms** or molecules are arranged in different ways. The most stable allotrope is called crystalline hexagonal selenium, which is a metallic grey colour. Crystalline monoclinic selenium is deep red, and 'amorphous' selenium is black or red when powdered. Selenium is a **semiconductor** that is sensitive to light. It burns in air to produce selenium dioxide, SeO_2, which is a very smelly solid, but it does not react with water or dilute acids.

▼ *This technician is adding a layer of white plastic to a glass plate coated with selenium. The plate will be used instead of photographic film to make a detailed X-ray photograph in a hospital.*

Extraction of selenium

There are minerals that contain selenium, such as berzelianite (copper selenide, CuSe) and clausthalite (lead selenide, PbSe). However, these are rare so most selenium is made as a by-product of copper **refining**. Selenium was originally extracted from the dust in the waste gases produced when copper sulphide **ores** were processed. Most selenium is now produced from the waste made when copper is refined by **electrolysis** or from the waste made by sulphuric acid manufacture.

Selenium in the diet

Selenium is an essential element in our diet, and our diet usually provides enough of it. Selenium is found in **enzymes** that our bodies make to protect our cells from chemical damage. People who do not get enough selenium suffer heart problems and muscle pain. Sheep and cattle raised in areas where the soil contains very little selenium develop 'white muscle disease', which causes difficulty in walking and sudden heart failure. To avoid soil deficiency, selenium can be added to fertilizers, and it can also be used as a dietary supplement for humans and animals.

Like many substances needed by the body, selenium can be poisonous in large amounts. A normal balanced diet is extremely unlikely to have too much selenium in it, but people who work with it or deliberately take a lot of selenium tablets may suffer from selenosis. In mild cases, sufferers get **brittle** hair and deformed nails, and in severe cases they lose feeling and control of their arms and legs. Some soils contain enough selenium to produce serious effects on grazing animals. In the USA, a plant called loco weed concentrates selenium, and livestock feeding on these plants can be poisoned.

Selenium sulphide, Se_2S_6, is a bright red-yellow powder that does not dissolve in water. It is used in anti-dandruff shampoos. Although selenium sulphide is very toxic, it is considered to be safe to use in shampoos because it does not get absorbed through the skin. Selenium and its **compounds** have many other uses including glass-making, **pigments** and electronic components and metal production. About 1600 tonnes of selenium are used in the world each year, some of it recycled from old photocopier and laser printer drums.

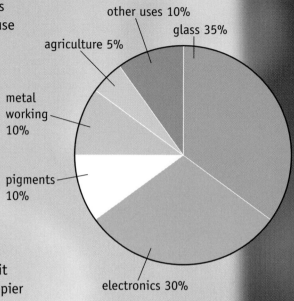

other uses 10%
glass 35%
agriculture 5%
metal working 10%
pigments 10%
electronics 30%

This pie chart shows the ▲ proportion of selenium used for different applications.

Glass and pigments

The biggest single use for selenium and its compounds is in glass-making. Ordinary bottle glass has a green tint caused by iron impurities in it. Selenium and selenium compounds can decolourize the glass by reacting with the impurities. However, the treated glass gradually turns an amber colour because selenium compounds are sensitive to light.

Glass can be deliberately tinted using metal selenites and selenates (selenium compounds which contain oxygen and a metal) to produce red, orange or yellow glass. This glass can be used for stained glass windows in cathedrals, offices and public buildings, and as decorative glass for works of art. Selenium compounds are also used in architectural glass for buildings, as they reduce the amount of heat and light passing through the glass.

Compounds containing selenium, sulphur and cadmium are also used in pigments for **ceramics**, plastics and paint. They make very stable pigments that keep their colour even when exposed to chemicals, high temperatures or ultraviolet light.

Electronics

Selenium is a **semi-conductor**. This means that it is an electrical insulator at room temperature, but a conductor when it is warmed up or tiny amounts of other elements are added to it. Selenium is used in rectifiers, which are semi-conductor devices that convert ac electricity (alternating current – the sort of electricity that comes from the mains) to dc electricity (direct current – the sort of electricity that is supplied by batteries). Devices that use rechargeable batteries, such as laptop computers, are connected to the mains using transformers that contain rectifiers. Selenium is also used in voltage surge protectors, which are devices that protect computers and other sensitive equipment from spikes in the electricity supply. Although other semi-conductor materials such as silicon, tellurium and gallium are beginning to replace selenium in electronic devices, it is still the second most important use of selenium.

Selenium is also sensitive to light. It can convert light directly into electricity, and it conducts electricity better when it is exposed to light. This means that selenium can be used in solar cells and camera exposure meters, and in the light-sensitive drums of photocopiers and laser printers. Other electronic uses include infrared detectors and X-ray receptors for medical imaging.

◀ *In buildings with a lot of glass, the glass often contains selenium to reduce the amount of heat and light that passes through.*

CHAPTER 6

Tellurium

Tellurium was discovered in 1782 by the Transylvanian chief inspector of mines, Franz Müller, who carefully analysed a bluish **ore** of gold. However, it was sixteen years later that a German chemist, Martin Klaproth, actually isolated the new **element**. He suggested its name, which comes from the Latin word for Earth.

Properties of tellurium

Tellurium is a metallic-looking silvery white solid, which is very **brittle** and easily broken up. It also forms a dark grey powder. Tellurium burns in air with a green-blue flame to produce tellurium dioxide, but it does not react with water or dilute acids and alkalis. However, molten tellurium corrodes metals such as copper, iron and stainless steel. It is a **semi-conductor** that is sensitive to light.

Tellurium itself is not very toxic, but exposure to it does have some very unpleasant side effects. These include a dry, metallic taste in the mouth, stomach upsets and tiredness. However, the worst side effect must be 'tellurium breath'. Tellurium is converted in the body into a chemical called dimethyl telluride, which causes body odour and foul breath similar to powerful garlic. Tellurium **compounds** are toxic. They can damage the kidneys and nerves, and cause changes in behaviour. Just 2 g of sodium tellurite is a lethal dose. Luckily, most of us are very unlikely to come into contact with a lot of tellurium. However, it must be handled extremely carefully when it is used in factories or laboratories.

Extraction of tellurium

Tellurium is sometimes found in its native state as a free element, but it is usually found in various **ores**, such as calaverite (gold telluride, $AuTe_2$) and coloradoite (mercury telluride, $HgTe$). The main deposits of tellurium ores are found in North America, Peru and Japan. As with selenium, most tellurium is made from the waste made when copper is refined by **electrolysis**. The waste contains copper telluride, Cu_2Te, and tellurium is extracted from it in three main stages.

These pieces of tellurium look shiny and metallic, but tellurium is very brittle and easily broken. Tellurium also forms a dark grey powder.

In the first stage, the waste is heated in air with sodium carbonate. This converts the copper telluride into sodium tellurite, which is a highly toxic compound of sodium, tellurium and oxygen. In the second stage, sulphuric acid is added to the sodium tellurite. This causes solid tellurium dioxide to form, which is filtered off ready for the last stage. In the final stage, the tellurium dioxide is dissolved in sodium hydroxide. Electricity is passed through the solution, which causes the tellurium dioxide to split into its two elements, tellurium and oxygen. The tellurium is sold as lumps, ingots and slabs, or as a fine grey powder.

About 220 tonnes of tellurium are used in the world each year for electronic components and the chemical industry. Most tellurium is used in metal production.

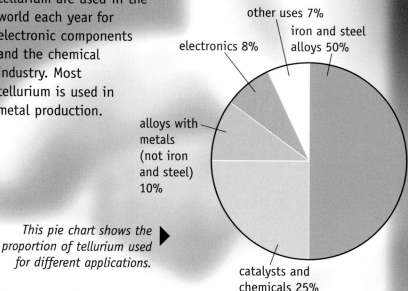

other uses 7%

iron and steel alloys 50%

electronics 8%

alloys with metals (not iron and steel) 10%

catalysts and chemicals 25%

This pie chart shows the proportion of tellurium used for different applications. ▶

Metal production

Tellurium is added to other metals to form **alloys** that have better properties than the metals alone. The biggest single use of tellurium is in making free-machining steel and copper. These are metals that are much easier to cut and shape than ordinary metals, which saves time and increases the life of the tools used on them. Very little tellurium is needed to do this – free-machining steel may contain just 0.04 per cent tellurium.

Cast iron contains iron carbide, a compound of iron and carbon called 'chill' by metal workers. Tellurium is used to control chill in cast iron. Iron carbide forms crystals in the metal and these crystals affect the properties of the cast iron. Tellurium is added to the metal to control the growth of these crystals, improving the **malleability** of the metal and making it easier to work into shape.

Lead is a soft metal, and adding tellurium to it increases its hardness and strength. Lead containing tellurium also resists attack by sulphuric acid better than lead alone.

Thermoelectric generators

Tellurium is used in thermoelectric generators. These are devices that convert heat directly into electricity. In a typical generator, gas burners heat up one side of a stack of **semi-conductors** containing tellurium and other **elements**, such as lead and tin. The other side is kept cool so that there is a temperature difference of up to 400 °C between the two sides. The stack of semi-conductors, called the thermopile, generates electricity as a result.

Solar cells and radiation detectors

Solar cells are devices that convert light (usually sunlight) directly into electricity. The best solar cells contain gallium indium phosphide or gallium arsenide. They can convert sunlight into electricity at 32 per cent efficiency. This means that only about a third of the energy in the sunlight is converted into electrical energy. Although solar cells made from cadmium telluride are only about 16 per cent efficient, they are much cheaper and so are used more widely. A related material, mercury cadmium telluride, is used in infrared (heat) detectors.

◀ *This calculator is powered by a solar cell that converts light into electricity.*

Other uses

Natural rubber is very soft as its molecules can slide past each other easily. If chemical bonds are made between the molecules, they stabilize the rubber and improve its properties. This process is called vulcanization, and both tellurium and sulphur are used in the manufacture of vulcanized rubber. Tellurium is used as a **catalyst** in the chemical industry, for example, to control **reactions** that produce artificial fibres. It is also an ingredient in blasting caps or detonators for explosives.

CHAPTER 7

Polonium

Marie Curie was a Polish–French physicist and chemist who was born in 1867. While studying uranium and its **ore**, pitchblende (which contains uranium oxide), she discovered that the pitchblende was more **radioactive** than the uranium itself. She realized that there had to be another **element** in the pitchblende that was more radioactive than uranium. Marie set out to isolate it from pitchblende with help from her husband, Pierre. In 1898, they managed to produce a mixture containing a new, radioactive substance mixed with an element called bismuth. They called the new substance polonium after Poland, where Marie was born.

The Curies set out to separate the polonium from the bismuth, but they never did succeed. This is because polonium turns rapidly into lead in a process called radioactive decay. The most common isotope of polonium has a half-life of 138 days, which means that during every 138 days, half of the polonium decays into another element. This meant that the polonium disappeared quicker than the Curies could isolate it!

Properties of polonium

Polonium is a silvery metal, which is a solid at room temperature. It dissolves well in dilute acids, but only slightly in alkalis. Polonium is intensely radioactive and highly toxic, so it is carefully controlled. The maximum dose allowed for a worker handling polonium is equivalent to about 7 billionths of a milligram! However, as it is so very rare, it is not normally a hazard. Unfortunately for Marie Curie, she worked with it at a time when the dangers of radiation were not known. She died of leukaemia in 1934, probably due to her exposure to radiation. Marie Curie's notebooks are still so radioactive that even today they have to be kept locked away in lead-lined containers!

Marie Curie, shown here in her laboratory in 1908, coined the term radioactivity to describe the rays given off by uranium. She won a second Nobel Prize in 1911, for discovering the elements radium and polonium.

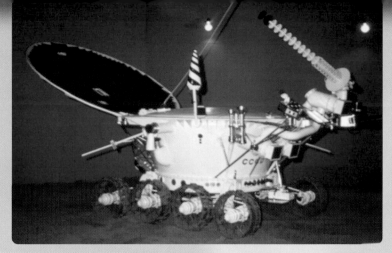

▲ Lunokhod I *was the first lunar rover. It was launched by the Russians in 1970, and travelled over 10 km on the Moon's surface. Its delicate scientific equipment was kept warm using heat from polonium.*

Extraction of polonium

Polonium is incredibly rare. There is only about one ten thousandth of a gram of it in a tonne of pitchblende. By comparison, a tonne of sludge from copper **refining** might contain several kilograms of tellurium and selenium. As a result, polonium is not made from pitchblende. Instead, bismuth is bombarded with neutrons to cause a nuclear reaction that makes polonium in milligram amounts. The polonium is then separated from the bismuth by **fractional distillation**.

Uses of polonium

There are only a few uses for polonium, and it must be carefully sealed and controlled to protect the users. It is used in anti-static brushes to remove dust from photographic film, and it is used to reduce the build-up of static electricity in textile factories and paper rolling mills.

Polonium produces a lot of alpha radiation, which causes the air to glow blue around larger pieces of the metal and the metal to become very hot. Satellites and space probes in the 1960s used polonium to keep their delicate instruments warm. Polonium was also used in radioisotope thermoelectric generators (RTGs). These are lightweight generators that convert heat electricity for satellites and other space craft. Modern RTGs usually use plutonium instead of polonium because it lasts longer.

The table below contains some information about the properties of the **elements** in group 6.

Element	Symbol	Atomic number	Melting point (°C)	Boiling point (°C)	Density (g/cm³)
oxygen	O	8	−218.3	−182.9	0.0013
sulphur	S	16	115	445	1.96
selenium	Se	34	221	685	4.82
tellurium	Te	52	450	988	6.24
polonium	Po	84	254	962	9.20

Compounds

These tables show you the chemical formulas of most of the **compounds** mentioned in the book. For example, carbon dioxide has the formula CO_2. This means it is made from one carbon **atom** and two oxygen atoms, joined together by chemical **bonds**.

Sulphides

Sulphides	formula
carbon disulphide	CS_2
hydrogen sulphide	H_2S
iron sulphide	FeS
lead sulphide	PbS
mercury sulphide	HgS
selenium sulphide	Se_2S_6
zinc sulphide	ZnS

Oxides

Oxides	formula
aluminium oxide	Al_2O_3
barium oxide	BaO
barium peroxide	BaO_2
calcium oxide	CaO
carbon dioxide	CO_2
carbon monoxide	CO
chromium oxide	Cr_2O_3
hydrogen peroxide	H_2O_2
iron oxide	Fe_2O_3
manganese dioxide	MnO_2
mercury oxide	HgO
nitrous oxide	N_2O
selenium dioxide	SeO_2
sulphur dioxide	SO_2
sulphur trioxide	SO_3
tellurium dioxide	TeO_2
uranium oxide	UO_2
vanadium(V) oxide	V_2O_5
water	H_2O

Sulphates

Sulphates	formula
ammonium sulphate	$(NH_4)_2SO_4$
calcium sulphate	$CaSO_4$
copper sulphate	$CuSO_4$
iron sulphate	$FeSO_4$
magnesium sulphate	$MgSO_4$
sodium sulphate	Na_2SO_4
zinc sulphate	$ZnSO_4$

Other compounds

Other compounds	formula
ammonium perchlorate	NH_4ClO_4
ammonium phosphate	$(NH_4)_3PO_4$
calcium carbonate	$CaCO_3$
calcium hydrogencarbonate	$Ca(HCO_3)_2$
calcium phosphate	$Ca_3(PO_4)_2$
ethanol	C_2H_5OH
glucose	$C_6H_{12}O_6$
magnesium carbonate	$MgCO_3$
nitroglycerine	$C_3H_5N_3O_9$
potassium chlorate	$KClO_3$
potassium nitrate	KNO_3
sodium hydroxide	$NaOH$
sodium sulphite	Na_2SO_3
sodium tellurite	Na_2TeO_3
sodium thiosulphate	$Na_2S_2O_3$

Acids

Acids	formula
carbonic acid	H_2CO_3
nitric acid	HNO_3
phosphoric acid	H_3PO_4
sulphuric acid	H_2SO_4
sulphurous acid	H_2SO_3
vitamin C (ascorbic acid)	$C_6H_8O_6$

Glossary

allotropes two or more different forms of an element. Allotropes have the same chemical properties but different physical properties.

alloy mixture of two or more metals, or mixture of a metal and a non-metal. Alloys are often more useful than the pure metal on its own.

antioxidant substance that prevents oxygen reacting with other chemicals

atom smallest particle of an element that has the properties of that element. Atoms contain smaller particles called sub-atomic particles.

atomic number the number of protons in the nucleus of an atom. It is also called the proton number. No two elements have the same atomic number.

bond force that joins atoms together

brittle word that describes a solid that breaks into small pieces when hit.

carbohydrate compound that contains carbon, hydrogen and oxygen atoms. Sugars, starch and cellulose are carbohydrates.

catalyst substance that speeds up reactions without getting used up

ceramic tough solid made by heating clay and other substances to high temperatures in an oven. Plates, bathroom tiles and toilet bowls are made from ceramics.

combustion any chemical reaction in which heat is produced, usually by a fuel reacting with oxygen in the air

compound substance made from the atoms of two or more elements, joined together by chemical bonds. Compounds can be broken down into simpler substances and they have different properties from the elements in them. For example, water is a liquid at room temperature, but it is made of two gases hydrogen and oxygen.

decomposition type of chemical reaction where a compound breaks down into simpler substances, such as the elements in them. For example, water can decompose to make hydrogen and oxygen.

electrode solid that conducts electricity, such as graphite or a metal. Electrodes are used in electrolysis.

electrolysis breaking down or decomposing a compound by passing electricity through it. The compound must be molten or dissolved in a liquid for electrolysis to work.

electron sub-atomic particle with a negative electric charge. Electrons are found around the nucleus of an atom.

element substance made from one type of atom. Elements cannot be broken down into simpler substances. All substances are made from one or more elements.

enzyme catalyst made by living things. Enzymes are made from proteins, and control the chemical reactions that happen in living things.

exothermic reactions that give out heat energy

fermentation reaction caused by the enzymes in tiny fungi called yeast. In fermentation, sugar is broken down to make alcohol and carbon dioxide.

fertilizer chemical that gives plants the elements they need for healthy growth

fossil fuels fuels made from the ancient remains of dead animals or plants. They are non-renewable fuels because once they run out, they cannot be replaced. Coal, oil and natural gas are fossil fuels.

fractional distillation type of distillation that is used to separate mixtures of two or more liquids. It works because different liquids have different boiling points.

fungicide chemical that kills the fungus that can damage crops

groups vertical columns of elements in the periodic table. Elements in a group have similar properties.

insecticide chemical that kills the insects that can damage crops

malleable word that describes a solid that can be bent into shape without breaking. Metals and alloys are malleable.

mineral substance that is found naturally but does not come from animals or plants. Metal ores and limestone are examples of minerals.

neutralization reaction between an acid and an alkali or a base. The solution made is neutral, which means it is not acidic or alkaline.

neutron sub-atomic particle with no electric charge. Neutrons are found in the nucleus of an atom.

nucleus the part of an atom made from protons and neutrons. It has a positive electric charge and is found at the centre of the atom.

ore contains minerals from which metals can be taken out and purified

oxidation adding oxygen to an element or compound in a chemical reaction. For example, carbon is oxidized when it reacts with oxygen to make carbon dioxide.

period a horizontal row of elements in the periodic table

periodic table the table in which all the known elements are arranged into groups and periods

photosynthesis chemical reaction that green plants use to make sugars from carbon dioxide and water using the energy from light. Oxygen is also made.

pigment solid substance that gives colour to a paint. Pigments do not dissolve in water.

polymer large molecule made from lots of smaller molecules (monomers) joined together. Plastic is a polymer.

product substance made in a chemical reaction

proton sub-atomic particle with a positive electric charge. Protons are found in the nucleus of an atom.

radiation energy such as X-rays and gamma rays, or fast-moving particles from the nucleus

radioactive word for elements that produce radiation

reactions chemical changes that produce new substances

reduction taking away oxygen from an element or compound in a chemical reaction. For example, iron oxide is reduced to iron when it reacts with carbon.

refining removing impurities from a substance to make it more pure. It can also mean separating the different substances in a mixture, for example, in oil refining.

respiration chemical reaction used by living things to release energy from food

roast to heat strongly for a long time

sacrificial protection method used to stop iron and steel rusting using a more reactive metal such as zinc

semi-conductor a substance, such as silicon, that is an electrical insulator at room temperature, but a conductor when it is warmed or other elements are added to it

Timeline

sulphur discovered	antiquity	unknown
air contains at least two different gases	1641	John Mayow
two gases are called 'foul air' and 'fire air'	1772	Carl Scheele
oxygen is made by heating mercury oxide	1774	Joseph Priestley
fire air is called oxygen	1774	Antoine Lavoisier
tellerium discovered	1782	Franz Müller
tellerium isolated	1798	Martin Klaproth
selenium discovered	1817	Jöns Berzelius
polonium discovered	1898	Marie Curie and Pierre Curie
ununhexium first made	1999	Lawrence Berkeley National Laboratory

Further reading and useful websites

Books

Bethell, Andy; Dexter, John; Griffiths, Mike, *Coordinated Science, Chemistry* (Heinemann Library, 2001)

Fullick, Ann, *Science Topics: Chemicals in Action* (Heinemann Library, 1999)

Knapp, Brian, *The Elements S* series, particularly, *Oxygen*; *Sulphur* (Atlantic Europe Publishing Co, 1996)

Oxlade, Chris, *Chemicals in Action* series, particularly *Atoms*; *Elements and Compounds* (Heinemann Library, 2002)

Websites

WebElements™
http://www.webelements.com
An interactive periodic table crammed with information and photographs.

DiscoverySchool
http://school.discovery.com/students
Help for science projects and homework, and free science clip art.

Proton Don
http://www.funbrain.com/periodic
The fun periodic table quiz!

BBC Science
http://www.bbc.co.uk/science
Quizzes, news, information and games about all areas of science.

Creative Chemistry
http://www.creative-chemistry.org.uk
An interactive chemistry site with fun practical activities, quizzes, puzzles and more.

Mineralology Database
http://www.webmineral.com
Lots of useful information about minerals, including colour photographs and information about their chemistry.

Index

Titles in the *Periodic Table* series include:

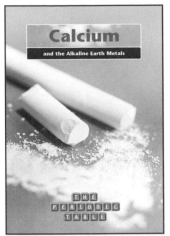

Hardback   0 431 16981 0

Hardback   0 431 16982 9

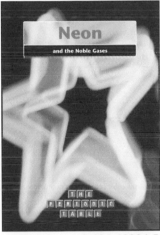

Hardback   0 431 16984 5

Hardback   0 431 16983 7

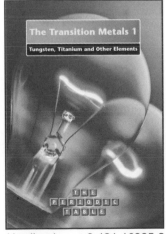

Hardback   0 431 16985 3

Hardback   0 431 16980 2

Find out about the other titles in this series on our website www.heinemann.co.uk/library